Anti-Crisis Analytics

Business Analytics that Helps
Before, During, and After a Crisis

Lev Kuandykov

ISBN-10: 151200930X
ISBN-13: 978-1512009309

SUMMARY

Evolution forces companies to search for new means of competition. Information technology, management science, and process knowledge are no longer enough to differentiate your business and stay competitive. Business executives often suffer from poor forecasts, insufficient data, and misleading advice that directs them towards imprudent decisions. Eventually, they find their businesses unprepared for yet another crisis and they ultimately fail.

This book is about business analytics - a new competitive advantage for companies. In it, Kuandykov describes the methods that will help your business stay ahead of its rivals, foresee future crises, survive them, and move on after them. The book is written in a plain language and is aimed at a broad audience. Readers will enjoy its fresh view on business analytics methods, its real world examples, and its useful hints and ideas for their work. The book is sure to be an invaluable resource for a broad range of business disciplines.

TABLE OF CONTENTS

Introduction

Part I. Before the Crisis

Part II. The Crisis

Part III. After the Crisis

One More Thing: Your Business Analytics

Introduction

CHAPTER 1

TREE OF COMPETITION

I discovered data science late in my career. The term was just emerging, and even today it may not resonate in most people's minds. 'Science' and 'Data' – both words evoke associations with Einstein, Star Trek, and Google. How about Business Analytics? The term is much more familiar. At least the term sounds comfortable – it simply means analytics for business. This book is about business analytics and economic crisis. This book is about analytics that will help you prepare your business for a crisis, and not only survive, but also thrive in the aftermath of a crisis. You don't need to have any prior knowledge of analytics to understand this book. Your business is what you know best!

Before we raise the curtains on applying analytics to your business, take the time to look around at the environment that your business operates in, including a detailed look at your competitors. There is an old saying: 'it doesn't matter how fast you're moving if you're moving in the wrong direction'. Even always moving sharks take time to adjust their trajectories. Stop and look around at your competitors and what they're doing. If you have been operating your business for some time you already have a good sense of the environment that you are currently operating in, but do you know how will it change in the next few years? How will you become a leader in this new environment?

The best way to see the big picture of business competition is to draw a tree. A tree of business life. Let's call it a tree of competition. To compete, you need to have something that others don't. Something to offer the customer, something that beats the offerings of your rivals, something that makes you stand out. The process of creating this magic 'something' has evolved over the history of business competition. Not continuously, but radically, and it caused major crises, which in turn accelerated business cycles. What was measured in centuries is now measured in months, leaving rings on the Tree of Competition.

The Tree of Competition grows over time. The top branches are where you are now, but the roots are buried in the soil of ancient times. We'll start with the roots. What did business competition look like a thousand years ago? People were making goods with their own hands and competing with each other by crafting the most attractive goods. Goods carried the name of the master who made them – much like todays brands, except the goods were unique. A vase, or a dress, or a tool … whatever it was, it was state of the art. To be competitive, goods had to be beautiful, practical and, probably, precious. This practice lasted for a long time until the industrial revolution.

The industrial revolution arrived with the invention of mass production. The human touch in manufacturing was sacrificed for availability and affordability and instead the conveyer belt became a symbol of the industrial revolution. Mass production began long before Henry Ford starting building Model Ts. The first mass production began in Napoleonic times when the French Emperor fostered innovation and financially supported the development of the loom. Ironically, weavers fanned the flame of revolution that consumed the city of Lyon, France's weaving capital, and eventually burned the French monarchy. The industrial revolution caused the first devastating crisis on our tree of competition. The intensity of the crisis was unprecedented, causing revolutions and wars and taking the lives of a million people.

In the early 20th century, Ford's assembly line was established and was representative of the modern concept of mass production. The popularity of labor division and machine- assisted processes skyrocketed, however it was often misused and overused. Charlie Chaplin, playing an assembly-line worker in the film Modern Times, eventually become insane because of his monotonous, repetitive work. However, while industry was booming, competition actually stagnated. It was time to invent a smarter way of operating and so the science of management emerged.

Nowadays, lot of schools teach management science and business operations. Master of Business Administration (MBA) programs, once an exclusive offering for business executives, is now a common academic discipline. Harvard, MIT Sloan, Warton, Yale, to name a few, graduate thousands of smart, highly educated young business leaders who can crack your complex marketing problem in a blink of an eye. The business schools tailor their programs to every industry and student budget. Full-time two-year programs, two-day or two-week courses, books, video recordings ... Delivery of business education is now more readily available as a means of helping you manage your business effectively. The "Effective Manager" has now become a cliché.

How does management science differ from the conveyer belt? This is another growth season for our Tree of Competition. The conveyer style of management became insufficient to compete, because everyone started using it and implementing similar ideas. Those who started practicing management science in their business operations became industry leaders, but only for a while. Once it was rare for a modern company to require a higher degree of business education for its managers. Companies that did, got ahead. But having MBAs on the board is no longer a competitive advantage. The clocks have started ticking faster. Humans cannot control the increasing speed of modern conveyers. Computers now rule the roost.

Information technology has pressed industry's accelerator pedal to the floor. Modern corporations operate at the speed of light. Literally. Enterprise resource planning systems like SAP process orders through the supply chain almost instantly. Everything is linked, and communications has taken on a new meaning. The business world has become truly global and mobile. A new class of electronic products has opened new markets that the ancients could never imagine. Consumers buy Angry Birds for their mobile devices using invisible bank transactions. Could you ever explain that to an artisan-craftsman creating a vase in ancient Greece? Today's industry is unworkable without computer and information technology – technology that operates via electronic signals, with digital information, with data. Those who have no control over their data face the risk of going out of business. Data has become the new currency, a real thing, like air and water. Needless to say, that data is everywhere. Computers and information technology do not provide a competitive advantage any more. Competition is saturated. We fight for resources, again, and are falling into an instant crisis. Why? Is it possible that the competition has exploited all the means of production? The answer is 'no'. We are simply entering into another transition.

Ancient craftsmen wouldn't be able to imagine steam machinery and electric conveyers. The weavers in Lyon could not imagine modern corporate management tools. Henry Ford could not imagine the Internet. And we cannot think about the future of competition. Or can we?

Computers have brought data to life. They can do things than human brains can't. Today, we can say that global industry works at the fastest pace possible. We all have conveyors, we all have good managers, we all have information technology in place. The wheel cannot spin faster. Every business has adopted the best practices of modern technology. Who can truly stay competitive in this environment?

The answer: Those who conquer the market first and capture the largest market share. Being first to market does not just prove your competitiveness. It means being ahead of your competition. It means you get to write the rules of the game. Think of the wording: saying 'come first' is much different than saying 'stay competitive'. If you dive deeper, then you'll realize that the dynamics, the moves towards business success, cannot happen in darkness. You need to understand where the wind blows, understand what the next big thing will be. You have to have insight and foresight, the searchlights that will show you the path. In the world of data, analytics is your searchlight. Those who foster business analytics will come to market first. They will know what will happen ahead of time, because they analyzed the data and won the battle before it started. Business analytics is the new weapon in the Art of War. Quite naturally, business analytics has become a hit, the next big thing.

CHAPTER 2

THE PRICE OF DECISION

Competition forces companies adopt new paradigms, evolve, and even radically change the ways they do business. Competition urges companies to use conveyers, management science, information technology, and business analytics. At the end of the day, the most critical recipe for company success is a combination of right decisions and right execution. The paradigms we mentioned above are just tools for achieving excellence in decision-making and execution. As the modern industry moves forward, 'doing the right things' – Peter Drucker's famous saying – morphs into 'making right decisions'. Eventually, having perfect execution capabilities and making the right decisions is what will help a company succeed. The data we collect, the market surveys, the business operation records, financial reports, all the other sources of information we use all support one major goal – to make the right decisions. We are willing to spend sleepless nights, work extra hours and even cheat (not you, but some of the Wall Street dealers) to make right decisions. In other words, we are willing to pay the price.

But what price?

Let's use a simple example to understand the price of a decision. Imagine you want to take a weekend trip with your family. You expect sunny weather for the next two days. You take a volleyball net and a barbeque set, and forget the raincoats and umbrellas. You go for the vacation, play volleyball with your family, prepare the barbeque … but then the weather changes. It starts to rain. Showers of rain. What if you knew in advance that that would happen? You would definitely have packed the umbrella.

Rain may not sound like a big deal. So let's imagine you're on a boat trip. You're sailing on the sea. Before leaving, you hear on TV that the weather will be perfect, but now you face a real thunderstorm. You relied on an inadequate forecast, and made a wrong decision. In the worst- case scenario, you could die, all because of a decision based on a faulty weather forecast. In these circumstances, the price you pay for your wrong decision is the price you would rather pay for an accurate forecast. So, metaphorically speaking, the price of a decision is the price of the forecast. In order to compete, you'd like to decrease the price you pay for your decision by increasing the quality of the forecast. Business analytics aims to decrease the price you pay for the forecast, and hence decrease the price of the decision. Using business analytics, you can make better decisions at a lower price.

Major IT software vendors anticipated the growing need for business analytics solutions. Success stories about how business analytics decreased operation and development costs, predicted customer behavior, and helped to optimize resource allocation started leaking to the mass media. The adoption curve took off in 2007, when SAP acquired Business Objects, a company providing analytical tools, and Oracle got its hands on Hyperion's Crystal Ball, a user-friendly application widely used by marketers and financial analysts. The enterprise resource planning (ERP) giants understood that it was no longer enough to increase the performance of their solutions. They understood the necessity of enabling their software to predict and analyze data at a higher level. Their modern clients wanted to predict the market, predict sales, predict problems on the production line, predict as much as possible. Microsoft and IBM entered the business analytics market at about the same time. In 2008, Microsoft introduced its flagship database server, MS SQL Server 2008, with Analysis Module for business analytics, or, 'business intelligence' as Microsoft branded it. IBM entered the market even earlier with Cognos acquisition in 2007. In 2009, IBM acquired the makers of SPSS and received access to one of the world's best analysis software package. It tried to tie the term 'business analytics' to the IBM brand. Actually, Other system integrators also started to absorb companies that developed business analytics software. The reason was clear: it wasn't enough to just record the data any more. It was time to use that data to predict the future.

From the viewpoint of the Tree of Competition, it actually doesn't matter which company will dominate, the blue chip or a start-up. The facts about acquisition and analytics integration only highlights the trend. It shows where the industry is heading. Eventually, the most important thing is the rise of business analytics as a tool for making decisions.

Part I

Before the Crisis

CHAPTER 3

SIXTH SENSE

In a crisis, stock markets fall, interest rates inflate, and the economy collapses. Worst of all, most of us don't even see it coming. We know that crises happen from time to time, and we know that sooner or later another one will come. This is what our common sense tells us. But if we know that a crisis will come, why are most of us are in shock when it arrives? Because we never know exactly when the financial skies will fall.

We compare economic crisis with natural disasters like forest fires, hurricanes, or an earthquake. Most of us don't know when these will hit, but animals usually feel subtle environmental changes in advance. Wild animals are intuitive enough to recognize the signs of an earthquake before our sophisticated electronic machines register the first tremors. Sometimes, however, our animal instincts awaken and we start to feel something we cannot explain. We feel the fine matter of the universe and other human beings in ways we cannot describe. We call this a "sixth sense." Our sixth sense often guides us when we don't have enough information to make a rational or emotional decision. The sixth sense, developed as intuition, helps us make the right decisions.

We often ignore our sixth sense, and suppress it with overthinking and our doubts. We definitely don't trust the sixth senses of others or the recommendations they make based on their intuition. Our mind likes facts. We want information written in bold, and tables with numbers, charts and scores. But what if we could record sixth-sense signals as solid data? What if we could use it predict the next crisis? This may sound like science fiction or a baseless speculation, but it is not. Not at all. We have some facts to share here.

Over a course of years, a web service called FAStocks.com collected the stock preferences of nonprofessional traders. FAStocks was a free online service for stock portfolio optimization. It offered a method for building a balanced portfolio with a maximum expected rate of return and minimum price volatility. The service used up-to-date stock prices of 1,200 companies listed on the Fortune 2000 and S&P 500 exchanges. FAStocks was fully automated, charged with Harry Markowitz modern portfolio theory and used a genetic algorithm for portfolio optimization. Users entered the website, selected up to 10 companies they were interested in from the list of 1,200 companies and clicked a button to receive a balanced portfolio, or, literally, the optimal balancing of the assets they chose. After the optimization, the user received a free financial report while the website recorded the portfolio and the creation date. FAStocks recorded no personal user data and didn't require users to register. This was an anonymous and fair deal between the user and the website. In 2014, the Scandinavian Institute of Business Analytics (SCANBA) acquired FAStocks and analyzed its data.

What SCANBA discovered was intriguing. Over three years, users optimized about 20,000 stock portfolios. The company users chose most frequently for their portfolio was Apple. This was no a surprise. After all, is, well, Apple. The most striking result was the users' timing and frequency of their selection of Apple for their portfolios. We filtered out fluctuations in the number of website visits and called this frequency a 'SCANBA index'. Formally, the SCANBA index of a company for a certain period is the percentage of mentions of the company during that period. For example, if on a radio show the hosts mention 12 companies and mentions a particular company three times, the SCANBA index of that company during that radio show for that date would be 3 / 12 = 0.25 or 25%. If, in certain months, a website had a thousand visitors who created stock portfolios and two hundred of them selected a particular company, then for that month the SCANBA index of that company on that website would be 200 / 1000 = 0.2 or 20%. In general, the SCANBA index reflects people's interest in a certain object. This is not a citation index at all; it is vague and subtle, implicit. People may not even recognize that they are expressing their interest. The SCANBA index is a numeric record of the interest shown by the crowd in an object.

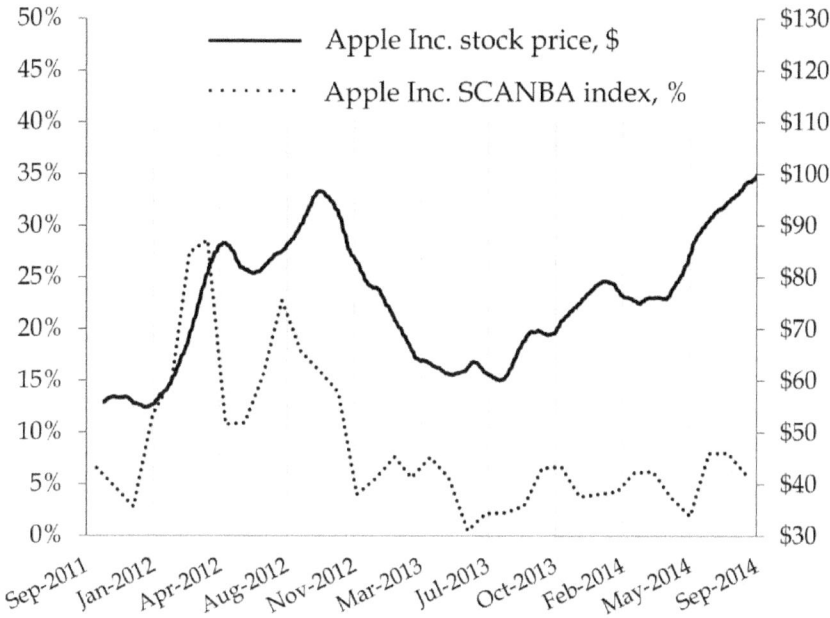

Look at the chart. The bold line is Apple's stock price (NASDAQ:AAPL day close), and the dotted line is Apple's SCANBA index calculated using FAStocks data for every month between September 2011 and September 2014. The curves behave similarly during the first two-year period, when Apple stock experienced two major rises and falls. Some may even notice similarities down the line, although they are less pronounced. The surprising fact is the similarity of the curves – between their major behavioral features, like peaks and valleys. The second surprise is the one- to two-month lag between the curves. The real mind-blowing observation is that the SCANBA index changes ahead of the stock price! In other words, if you know the

SCANBA index, or have data to calculate it, then you can predict changes in a stock price one or two months in advance. You can know whether the price change you see is a correction or a real turn. The SCANBA index indicates that interest of the public in a stock acts as a sort of sixth sense for traders.

This discovery is hard to believe – until you see the data. When we saw this chart for the first time, our rational minds resisted adopting the data, although our reason for acquiring FAStocks was to confirm this counterintuitive theory. The SCANBA index may feel like magic – even to me, its author – and it still retains a shade of mystery. However, traditional forecasting is not magic. It is a real thing called predictive analytics.

Let's move on, and continue to explore the power of predictive analytics in the business world.

CHAPTER 4

PATTERNS AND PREDICTIONS

In 2012, Nokia Research conducted a Mobile Data Challenge, a competition for data scientists intended to reveal the power of analytics as applied to smartphone data. The participants received access to cellphone locations, call lists, and the social-interaction logs of 200 volunteers collected over one year in and around Lausanne, Switzerland. De Domenico, Lima, and Musolesi won the contest. They developed an algorithm – a multivariate nonlinear timeseries prediction – so accurate that it could literally forecast where a person would be the next day. Their prediction method was accurate to within a few meters. In 2010, Mascaro, Korb, and Nicholson used Bayesian networks to spot unusual behavior of ships in Sydney Harbour by mining the harbour's vessel movement records. They were able to contrast suspicious patterns in ship movements against their typical trajectories in the harbor. In both examples, analytics predicted the future behavior of an object, person or a marine vessel, and detected deviations from the normal regime before a human observer could recognize it.

Patterns are attributes of established economies before a crisis. Patterns tend to become stronger over time when an environment remains stable. In the established economy, businesses are mature, trade channels are developed, social networks are established, markets are occupied, and the rules of the game are written. These rules define patterns, which are sometimes too complex to recognize with the naked eye, but transparent to data mining algorithms and forecasting methods.

The basic idea underlying all forecasting methods is that something regular and predictable is going on. This is called the signal. When something else is going on, something irregular and unpredictable, it is called noise. Every data set is a mix of signal and noise. Signals usually carry the information we care about. Noise is simply the discrepancy between the signal and the actual results. When you forecast, you are trying to separate the signal from the noise to find a pattern.

A common, though debatable, practice for finding patterns is to search for correlations between events. Correlations are a fundamental part of traditional forecasting such regression analysis, which is available in Excel. One may or may not like it, but correlations are key to understanding forecasts, and they play an important part in diagnosing how well your forecasts perform. Imagine you have two variables: sales revenue and advertising budget. You can express the strength of the relationship between the variables using a number called the correlation coefficient. Forecasters often use the squared value of the correlation coefficient, or the coefficient of determination, or simply 'R-squared'. The closer R-squared is to 1, the stronger the variables are linked. This is a common belief in traditional forecasting, and one that is often misused. The thoughtless fit of variables to explain a certain pattern often case an effect of a stripped thread. Predictive analytics is a masterpiece of data science, and you have to know the art of data analysis to use it wisely.

Variable, or 'factor' selection is a key step in pattern forecasting. In regression methods, picking the factors requires careful attention to several statistical metrics (such as coefficient of determination and statistical significance). In general, tuning the forecasting algorithm using factor selection is a tradeoff between its exploitative and explorative power. You can think of this as drawing a line through a cloud of points on a chart. The line is your forecast, something that explains the allocation pattern of the scattered points. You can draw a straight line through the scattered dots if you feel there is a trend. The resulting trend line will have high explorative power, since you can use it to forecast far ahead in the future, but you will miss the details. Alternatively, you can draw a snake-like curve that tries to capture all features in the point allocation, all fine deviations from the trend line. With this curve, you will get high exploitation power, but you can be fooled by the noise and may search for a pattern that does not exist. In other words, the forecasting algorithm tuned for exploitation can interpolate data within the data set, but if you want to make extrapolations and predict data far beyond the known range, then you need to increase the explorative power and sacrifice the details. In my experience of regression analysis, the rule of thumb was to keep less than five factors in a single regression fit. Of course, this rule is very subjective. However, the five-factor guideline was dictated by a philosophical principle credited to the medieval English logician, William of Occam, who opined: 'Entities should not be multiplied unnecessarily.' This famous principle is known as Occam's Razor, and it has a lot of modern reincarnations, including the well-known acronym, KISS, or 'Keep It Simple, Stupid.'

Statistical significance, often identified with p-value, is one of the metrics used to help a researcher pick the right factor. Typically, statisticians belong in one of two camps: Pearson's camp of 'classical' statistics, and the Bayesians. Bayesians fairly criticize the p-value metric, as it drives researchers to conclusions that implicitly refer to unobserved events. The generality and power of Bayesian statistics was developed by the genius of Pierre-Simon Laplace, a legendary French mathematician and astronomer, almost simultaneously with Thomas Bayes, an English minister and mathematician, who expressed his ideas of inference in 18th-century . But the wide adoption of statistical methods, and p-value in particular, is credited to Karl Pearson, an English professor at the turn of 20th century. The p-value metric is a handy tool for screening factors for regression forecasts. 'Just drop the factors with p-value below 0.05!' say average statisticians, without much thought.

To tune the forecast and increase the accuracy of

pattern predictions, we often tighten the parameters to unreasonable levels. This is the moment when the thread is stripped. We pick the wrong factors, we match noise with loose signals. Stop! Watch out! If you can predict everything in your business, if you think you have found all the correlations, if your R-squared is almost 1, then be ready for the crash. Prepare for the crisis! Stagnation of smooth growth is against nature.

CHAPTER 5

BLACK BOXES

Did you know that your credit limit is approved by a robot? (No, I'm not referring to your honest and friendly bank clerk.) The term 'robot' means a computer, a software program that recommends whether a credit manager should approve or disapprove your loan request based on your credit profile. Huge financial groups, like Citibank, which operate in commodity markets, must decide credit-line sizes in enormous volumes daily, even hourly. Think of a bank as a factory, a highly automated production line with a quality-control system controlled via a computer. The operator, the bank clerk, oversees the process and can only document the inputs and report the outputs. They cannot change the process. You submit your personal information to the bank, your age and marital status, your income, your car manufacturer, the name of your dog, whatever the bank will require in order to process your loan. The bank clerk feeds your profile info into a computer – a black box, a weird thing with unknown decision-making rules – that provides the clerk with an answer, which can also be weird. For example, a bank clerk might tell you that the bank has approved a $123,000 credit line for you. Where does this number come from? Well, we know the number came from the black box computer – but how was it calculated?

The black boxes encapsulate predictive algorithms, which are typically much more complex than Excel regressions. The algorithm is tuned (or 'trained', as data scientists say) to generate the best possible answers for a given situation. You deal with black boxes all the time. I bet you don't put much thinking into where the weather forecast comes from, or how movie theaters schedule show times. Most black boxes use historical data about the process and predictive algorithms to detect patterns and generate forecasts.

No doubt, the star of the black box algorithms is the Neural Network. There are other networks, too, such as

Bayesian networks. There are also learning trees, naïve Bayes, support vector machines (to name a few), but Neural Networks top the chart. The Net, as data scientists call it, is little better than other algorithms of the same class, as sometimes they do not predict at all. It is easy to spoil the Net by overtraining it; in which case its exploration power goes down. But the fact is that Nets exist in all software packages for predictive analytics.

The term 'Neural Network' was created in 1940s by researchers studying the principles of biological neural networks. Roughly speaking, the scientists tried to find a mathematical algorithm that could explain how our brains work. The full name of the Net is Artificial Neural Networks, since the core element of the Net is an artificial neuron, as an analogy to a biological nerve cell, or 'neuron'. In nature, biological neurons form a network that transmits electrochemical signals that enable us to think and move. The links between neurons have a special biological formation, a synapse, which holds or amplifies the signal between the neurons. In artificial neural networks, synaptic weights are the fitting parameters. You can think of these weights as regression coefficients. The difference with the regression is that the Nets can have a complex structure with a number of neurons organized in layers. The synaptic weight values are meaningless to the user, which is why the Net is a 'black box' algorithm: you cannot say anything just by looking the synaptic weights.

Neural networks can solve almost any pattern-prediction task. In 1989, a Japanese scientist, Ken-Ichi Funahashi, proved that an infinitely large neural network with one layer of neurons could approximate any continuous function. The Nets have a number of versions and there are tons of books written about their properties and usage. For us, the utility of black-box algorithms is in their predictive ability. When you are about to make a decision, every piece of information is critical. You can appeal to your experience, your gut feeling, but the most solid thing is data and the patterns that can be recognized in that data – the numbers that the predictive algorithm generates for you. Predictive analytics is a 'must-have' in the modern business world. The black boxes are your best friends when it comes to making decisions. The black-box algorithm can catch the most complex pattern, which you will miss with a regression. Potentially, the black box can tell you if something is wrong in your business long before a crisis occurs and whether your environment has deviated from the patterns you're used to – and thus foreshadow a crisis.

CHAPTER 6

MONITORING

Unless you can see through the numbers, you need a visual aid. Tables are the worst way to present data. Even today, vast majority of reports are filled with tables. Pivot tables? Whatever! Pivot tables are still tables. When you look at a table of numbers, your brain struggles to visualize it – to find minimums, maximums, scale, or draw a mental chart. Our brains just do not work with tables. When you deal with predictive analytics, visual representation of the data is an essential component. However, an overwhelmingly detailed infographic can be a bad thing, too. Be plain and clear. Read 'Presentation Zen' by Garr Reynolds, and if you already have read it, read it again. Watch David McCandless's TED talk, the 'Beauty of Data Visualization'.

Even if you don't have predictive analytics yet, your eyes can do a better job when they see a chart. This is sometimes called 'visual analytics'. Daimler, a well-known German car manufacturer, used bubble charts on top of their enterprise resource planning system to track project portfolio performance. In their book 'The Innovation Game', Corre and Mischke describe how the bubbles growing and moving along the chart gave valuable hints to Daimler management – by itself, the visual analytics information was valuable. A simple box and whisker plot will show you where the bulk of your scattered data sits, what the average is, and how it compares to other data sets. If your data visualization is strong, then you can spot patterns faster. The rule is simple: if there is a difference, then your eyes will capture it; if you can't see the pattern instantly, then there is no pattern. (Don't stare for too long.)

Business analytics is about using the right data, for the right people, at the right time. You are the right person, and today is the right time. You have to monitor your business. You have to have a reporting system, with a slick, cool look, one that's mobile and at your fingertips, with up-to-date data presented in bubble charts, box and whisker plots, histograms and maps. Your business data must flow through black boxes that predict patterns and trends, find clusters and deviations, and bring brilliant visualizations to your reporting system. Remember: forewarned is forearmed. Robust business analytics is your digital shield from crisis.

Part II

The Crisis

CHAPTER 7
YOUR RESOURCES

It's here, and it's wild and devastating. Walls topple around you, zombies kick at the doors, your hair turns gray in an instant and you're about to leap out the window. But wait! We're talking about the economy, not a scene in horror movie. The sun and the air are still there, your car is still in the driveway and your head – along with your brain and knowledge – is intact.

I spent a substantial part of my career with Corning, an industrial company with a 160-year-old history. Can you imagine how many economic crises it weathered over those 160 years? Survival during crisis is all about managing resources. Corporations approach crisis management strategically and execute what they call 'rings of defense'. The first ring of defense involves spending cuts, reduced production and setting tight hiring limits. The second ring is discontinuing contracts with temporary employees and reducing working hours. The third ring brings in early retirement plans, voluntary layoffs with bonuses and, the hardest part, involuntary layoffs. There is a fourth ring, too. It's the one that's not so obvious – the cuts to research and development. Why is R&D so important? Plenty of companies don't do any of it! True. But it's also true that companies without R&D usually don't last for 160 years.

Foregoing R&D is like living without thinking about your future, living without analytics, living without brains. The last thing you want to sell is your brain, your analytic system. Your assets will come and go. The way you organize, and how you manage, matters the most. If you think of an organization that has lasted for 160 years, what is its legacy? Plants? No. Products? No. People? Definitely not. The only things that last are the corporate culture, the management principles and rules of behavior. Analytics will not help you with your corporate strategy. Implementing business analytics is a strategy itself. Analytics will help you to organize and save your resources during a crisis, optimize spending, and improve business processes.

CHAPTER 8

THE VALUE-ADDED ANALYSIS PROCESS

Essentially, business is a process that converts inputs into outputs. Every business does that. In education, you convert newcomers into experts; in finance, you convert cash, assets and obligations into financial products; in any assembly industry, you convert parts into goods. The business process is a line of sequential steps that adds value to your product. What business owners usually want, especially during a crisis, is to make the production process cheaper and more efficient – in other words, to decrease the number of steps while retaining the product's value. Analytics can help you with that. Actually, if you are serious about your business and plan to withstand the crisis, business process analytics is your lifejacket. Never stop re-evaluating your business process, and always conduct value-added analysis.

Value-added analysis is a method to identify opportunities to eliminate waste and simplify a process. By doing a value-added analysis, you identify which steps add value and which ones don't, and gather information that can reveal opportunities to simplify the business process.

As we said, every process, large or small, is a series of steps, both value-added and non-value added. Every step adds cost and complexity, because it adds time, requires space, and creates inventory. Someone has to do the work, so there may be training involved. Maintenance might be needed. Every step is an opportunity to make a mistake. The challenge is to find the non-value added steps, eliminate the waste and, when possible, simplify the steps that actually add value. The more waste you eliminate, the better you will be financially, and the easier it will be to survive the crisis.

How does it work? You start by documenting current profits using a flow chart, spaghetti diagram, or other similar means. Then you record each step in the flow and identify them as value-added or non-value added. The results are reviewed, and by challenging every non-value added step and trying to eliminate it, you develop an improved process flow. Remember, value-added analysis is a very simple activity that often leads to surprising results, such as lower manufacturing costs. By eliminating unnecessary steps and streamlining the remaining ones, you will reduce lead times, have more capacity with low inventories, and so on. By eliminating steps, you reduce the chances of creating defects and improve quality. Eventually, you will substantially decrease your production costs, which in turn will allow you to decrease the product price while retaining the same profit margin.

Six steps lead to successful value-added analysis. First, you define the scope of the analysis. What are you analyzing? Where is the beginning and the end of the process? The second step is to decide who will participate in the analysis. Third, you create a process flow, a spaghetti diagram, or use another tool to chart the process flow. Fourth, you develop the ideal process flow, starting with only the value-added steps. The fifth step is to develop your proposed process flaw. The last step is, of course, to summarize the results in a final report with recommendations.

There are at least two concepts you need to remember

when doing value-added analysis. The first concept is the 'Three Types of Steps'. A Type One step changes the form, fit, or function of a product for the benefit of the customer. This is a value-added step. A Type Two step does not change the product for the benefit of the customer. That, of course, is the non-value added step. The Type Three step is a form of non-value added step that includes non-value added, but required, transactional tasks such as processing purchase orders, paying invoices, doing payroll, etc. These tasks are required for a business to operate because they enable the manufacturing process and the delivery of services, but for the purposes of a value-added analysis, they are considered as non-value added.

The other key concept or definition to keep in mind is the 'Eight Different Types of Waste'. Knowing them will help you find them. Of course, you can't find waste if you don't know what you're looking for. Business process analysts often use a mnemonic – HITIMWOOD – to help remember them. It stands for Human and Intellectual Capital Waste; Transportation Waste; Inventory Waste; Waste of Motion; Waste from Waiting; Waste of Overproduction and Over-processing; and Defects. I will not go into the details of each one, but it is key that you bear them in mind when you do a value-added analysis.

After you have identified the beginning and end of your process and who will participate in the analysis, you have to create a map of your current flow. Use symbols that help identify each step: profit steps, inventory points, delay, transportation, inspection, decisions. Next, with the process flow chart and data collected on that process, you do the analysis. A good practice is to record each steps and the data associated with it – such as distance, part size, time required. Then determine what steps are value-added and non-value added, and color them in different colors by type. Most likely, you will see that your current process is full of non-value added steps.

The next step in the value-added analysis process is to develop the ideal process flow — that is, starting with 100% value-added (only the two value-added steps). This ideal state is usually easy to construct, since it's only the value-added steps minus all the non-value added ones. A perfect process is seldom achieved, but the analysis helps the team stay focused on the value-added activities and creates a new, improved process flow.

Before each step, ask yourself and the team: What is the purpose of this step? Why is it necessary? Who does it and why? Where is it done? Those things will typically help you clarify the real intent of a step and whether you can eliminate it, combine it, or simplify it. After you have done your proposed process flow, summarize the impact of the changes. Summarize those as the number of steps eliminated, the number of non-value added steps before and after the analysis, distance traveled, and lead time, for example. There might be other factors you can add to your analysis, too.

CHAPTER 9

VALUE STREAM MAPPING

You can draw your business process as a flow chart. This is the ideal case. However, your knowledge of the process can be so vague – and you will be surprised at how vague it can be – that you just cannot draw a reasonable flow chart. But there is a whole process for documenting your business process. It's called Value Stream Mapping, or VSM. This technology is widely used in Lean Manufacturing and Six Sigma process quality-improvement efforts. The VSM can be literally drawn on a huge sheet of paper. You customers, plants, trucks, orders, financial forecasts, how they're all connected – it's basically a big picture of your business, and it's a great supplementary tool for starting a value-added analysis. The VSM yields invaluable information about your business process. Often, at least before a crisis hits, no one really looks at the process this way. Not everyone knows how the business actually works and operates. The VSM is a great way to gain a real understanding of what's happening behind the scenes, if you will.

If you read 'Learning to See', a book by Rother and Shook, you'll learn that a value-stream map is a pictorial representation of all the activities required to bring a product or service to a state of completion. When you map a process, what you're essentially doing is following the product or service's path from beginning to end. In other words, you literally go out on the shop floor, you talk to the operators and the experts who do the work, day in and day out. As you do that for each process step in a systematic, rigorous way, you collect data. The data you collect is basically a set of questions. You're going to be asking questions like: What are the triggers and authorizations for production at this step? What are the information flows? How long does this process take? Why? Ask questions about each process. For a manufacturing process, you'll ask about set-up times and changeovers and quality, and things like that. As you do this, you draw a visual representation of the material service and the information flows, and you think critically about what that current state is. You want to discover whether there are any problems, to understand each of those problems, and then start to explore what you might need to do to solve them. After you do the analysis of the current state, the idea is to then draw and design a "future state" map of how values should flow in the improved process. I make it sound simple, but it's really a lot of work.

If you are building a VSM for manufacturing, you want to be onsite and talk to the operators in the room. (Personally, I think the operators in a plant make a lot of sense.) But for transactional processes, where you don't have operators to talk to or manufacturing processes to put your hands on, I would recommend doing the VSM offsite. Getting people away from their offices helps them stay more focused on your subject. It's not uncommon to hold a value-stream mapping session as a workshop – and by workshop, I mean something for which you block off a significant segment of time. You should call in an objective facilitator to lead it. It could be someone with experience in your company, or an external consultant. Make sure that you have cross-functional representation. You always need the right group of people in the room. You might even incorporate some training and guidance about value stream mapping along the way. The workshop really helps a team come together around a common vision and mission.

When doing VSM, expect that a lot of people – or some people – may react negatively to what you find. Because as you dig deep and really turn some rocks, you're likely to discover some waste, and no one wants to be a process owner holding the bag full of waste. So it's important to make sure that when you do VSM that you're prepared for that debate.

There is no limit to how big or how small this process can be. Value stream maps take on all sorts of shapes and sizes. It's not the picture you draw that counts. That's just an tool for the analysis and the critical thinking that takes place. The end result must be an actual plan. This will allow a small or large group to see the business process as a whole, and relatively quickly determine where to focus their efforts. And, most importantly, to formulate a plan. Remember, the crisis has already has one foot in the door.

A common pitfall is to think of the map is the end point, when in fact it's really just the beginning. Sometimes you need an invention. Sometimes you need innovation. Sometimes you need to start with a new piece of paper and go to a design project. Sometimes you need to appeal to advanced analytics to re-design your process.

CHAPTER 10

REDESIGN

During a crisis, you can't run your business the same way you did before the crisis. This is obvious. You need to change – which, together with death and taxes, is one of three life's three inevitabilities. The taxes are up to you, but your business is not going to die! In order to change and keep your head above water, you need to understand your business process even better – whether you're an insurance company, in the steel industry, or a chain of coffee shops. You have to summon a good, old-fashioned process engineer to learn best practices and unite your team, or call a consulting company to draw a new value stream map to eliminate non-value-added steps and redesign. Maybe you will find bottlenecks in your process, like long queues and delays that irritate your customers and cause them to abandon you. You'll likely end up with several options – several new designs for your improved process – but only one chance to try one of them because of time and budget pressures. But how will you know that you picked the best version of the new process? How will you know whether you caught the devils in the details? No doubt, you will wonder if there was a way to model this process in a safe environment, like a sandbox or a computer. After all, there are plenty of computer games, such as SimCity, where the virtual world is not that far from reality. What if you could test your new process in a virtual world before investing in the full-scale deployment? So many questions! The only answer I can give you in this book is: "Use analytics!"

And on that front, there is a technology called imitation modeling, or discrete event modeling. The latter is an industry in itself, and includes a number of software vendors and consulting companies.

Let's take a closer look at the field.

The discipline that studies business processes is often called 'Operations Research'. This is a general term that encompasses a number of different techniques. Here, we must mention 'Business Dynamics', a book by Sterman. It's a thorough description of system dynamics, one of the most commonly used frameworks for modeling business processes such as plant operations and market behavior. System dynamics will help you draw and animate your value-stream maps, but the method can only deal with continuous processes and cannot capture individual system elements. (We'll talk about system dynamics in the next chapter.) Remember, you have no room for mistakes – your business is in crisis. You have to be sure of the details, so you want the best business process modeling possible.

Business process modeling grew up with the deployment of discrete-element methods. These were known for decades and, implicitly, pioneered by Carl Adam Petri with his Petri Networks. The wide adoption of his methods was limited by computer software availability. After the software appeared on the shelves, application of discrete event modeling, also known as simulation modeling, boomed (yes, imitation and simulation are the same thing). Laguna and Marklund wrote a reasonably good book on this called 'Business Process Modeling', where you can learn the basic notations and models.

The software packages for discrete event modeling make up a long list. It includes Arena, ExtendSim, SimProcess, and more. AnyLogic software is a standout. It combines both methods (system dynamics and discrete events) but also includes integrated agent-based modeling, and is fully customizable. When you decide to dive into discrete event modeling, I recommend reading 'The Big Book of Simulation Modeling', by Borshchev.

Business process modeling is a 'must-have' for all plants and warehouses. Most of Fortune 500 companies use it to test scenarios, optimize work schedules, optimize inventory allocation, and simply monitor their processes. A discrete element model of a plant is a full-scale replica of the plant that captures all the details: the movement of parts on conveyers, assembly lines with workers, warehouses with forklift trucks, etc. The model is literally a virtual plant on your desktop. All the model elements can interact and operate just as they happen in the real plant using real work schedules, maintenance schedules, stochastic breaks, etc. The degree to which the models can be refined is almost infinite.

A Moscow online retailer, Utkonos, used the discrete element model to optimize its warehouse. The warehouse was a multi-story building with an inventory of tens of thousands of items. Pallets of goods were delivered to the warehouse by trucks. Servicing staff unloaded and transported the pallets to the reception zone. Pallets were handled, marked by registrars and then moved to the storage zone using forklift trucks. A consulting company created a detailed virtual replica of all the trucks, forklifts, passages, elevators, piles and workers. The model was linked to the warehouse's management software for realistic source data. After the model was validated against the warehouse's key process indicators with 90% accuracy, the redesign work began. The new process tests were safe, because all the creativity was directed to the virtual world of the model. Eventually, the company was advised to reallocate the pallets and shut down a whole level in the building, partially because the elevators proved to be the efficiency bottleneck.

With models, you can evaluate performance of various process designs and crash-test the best of them. For example, your plant manager can learn what disruptions may occur in the workflow if the plant experiences certain delays with a spare-part supply, or what bottlenecks will appear in the process if the production output is doubled, etc. After the new process deployment and model validation, you can fine-tune your virtual process and transfer the new process parameters to the field. This part is called business process optimization. Your redesigned process will save you a lot. You will be literally flying – and crisis storm clouds seem far away when you're far above them.

CHAPTER 11

LIVING UNDER CONSTRAINS

Constraints stimulate creativity. During a crisis, your budget is a typical constraint. Not enough customers, not enough cash, not enough financial support from banks and investors. Actually, when your budget is tight, you have two options: to come up with a new creative solution through a business process redesign, or to carefully redistribute your resources, prioritize and optimize your budget allocation, and find an optimum balance. When your business is rich and fat, you can spend overspend. Life is good, so why bother to hold back? But during a crisis, every penny counts. And that's when budget optimization happens. People only do it when something forces them to. In your case, this something is the economic crisis.

If your advertising budget is low, then your sales are low. You want to see your sales grow, but you don't want to spend a lot on promotion. Optimization seeks to balance the tradeoffs you need to make. Speaking scientifically, in the promotion budget allocation, you want to maximize the effectiveness of your promotional efforts for a given budget. These are your objectives and constraints. Direct-mail marketing; ads in magazines, newspapers, and web; public relations activities and social network pages; radio and TV advertising; search engine marketing – these are your promotion vehicles. But how do you allocate your promotion budget across these different vehicles to maximize the number of ad impressions? In the world of analytics, we refer to situations of this type as 'optimization problems'. Optimization seeks to find maximum and minimum values for an expression called the objective function, subject to a set of constraints.

Ironically, lack of revenue may force you to seek ways to increase your profit with the same goods in same market conditions only by optimizing the price. Why you have not done this before? How do you set the price for your products? There is a whole sophisticated methodology around pricing. In general, consumers tend to buy more when the price is low, and vice versa. We are not talking about luxury goods – we're talking about frozen vegetables and pizza. They feel they can "stock up" at the lower prices in the short term. In the long term, they don't continue to buy because there's a limit to the amount of frozen vegetables they want to own, even when they're offered at very low prices. The bottom line is that you can sell more at lower prices, and eventually gain more, through sales volume in certain market environments. The fine balance you have to find is called the 'optimal price'. To find it, you have to collect data about your customer demand, conduct surveys, analyze past sales data, even conduct a market experiments and construct a demand curve (the number of goods consumers are ready to buy at a given price). Once you know a product or service's demand curve, you can find its optimal price. For each point on the demand curve, you can calculate the resulting revenue and cost. With known revenue and cost, you can calculate profits – just subtract the cost from the revenue. The optimal price is the price that gives you maximum profit at lowest cost. It's that simple.

Sorger, in 'Marketing Analytics', suggests conducting optimization of promotion and pricing activities using Excel Solver, a popular tool among marketers. Indeed, the tool will work, but you'll never know whether the solution it delivers is the best possible one. If your solution space looks like a simple parabola, with just one maximum or minimum, depending on how you look at it, then it's probably fine and you can safely do a basic optimization. However, what if your parameter space looks like the surface of an ocean and you have to find the highest wave? When you optimize the parameters of your redesigned process, you may have to adjust dozens, even hundreds of factors to improve your key performance indicators (KPI). To do that, you need two things: a process model, or a function that links your factors with your KPIs and the optimization algorithm.

There are plenty of optimization algorithms. You'll probably never encounter most of them, and none if your software is smart enough and has only one button ('Solve' or 'Optimize'). You don't have to be a control freak, but it's good to understand what happens behind the scenes during an optimization. There are local optimums and global optimums. Again, think of waves on an ocean surface. Some waves are high enough to suit your needs. If you're an average surfer, these are the local optimums. But if you want the biggest wave – not because you're desperate but because, like Mercedes, you prefer 'the best or nothing' –

you want the global optimum. This represents the best possible combination of your process parameters, the best possible price for your product, and the best possible allocation scheme for your promotional budget.

The optimization algorithms also operate in terms of exploitation and exploration, much like the algorithms of predictive analytics. Some algorithms are good for combinatorial optimization – for example, genetic algorithms, where the variants are coded in ones and zeros and cross over and mutate like genes in biology to exploit and explore the solution space. Others are good for continuous landscapes, like the search for hypothetical waves. For aesthetic reasons only, I want to describe an algorithm called a 'swarm', or more precisely, a 'particle swarm optimization'. Engelbrecht nicely covered it in his book 'Fundamentals of Computational Swarm Intelligence'. To sum up: one fine day, a psychologist and a mathematician were watching a flock of birds fly over a city square in search for food. The birds had a social and individual component in their behavior. The social component made them fly the same direction as their neighbors and maintain the integrity of the flock. The individual component permitted some birds to deviate from the general flock direction and explore adjacent areas. If one bird saw that its neighbor had found some food, it followed and eventually changed direction of the whole flock. Swarms and shoals also demonstrate similar behavior. The mathematician managed to create an equation so general that today it is successfully used to solve complex optimization problems. It can find global optimums faster than other techniques.

To conclude this chapter, I will repeat the well-known statement: there's always room for improvement (i.e., for optimization). So treat the crisis as an opportunity, be smart, and use analytics! Rise and shine!

Part III

After The Crisis

CHAPTER 12

WHAT IF...?

Talk to people. They are finally crawling out their caves, emerging from their shelters. Their Ark sits on top of a mountain, raised there by a flood – the one that washed away the previous world and all of previous civilization.

You learned your lesson. You knew you should have used predictive analytics before the crisis, and redesign and optimize your business as the crisis unfolded. God laughed at your plans and simply wiped out everything around you. The environment changed, you changed, they changed.

Fortunately, life sometimes allow you a global reset. Now you need to start from scratch, and you need some inputs. You already tortured yourself with questions: 'What if I'd held on to that contract?', 'What if I did that thing differently?', 'What if I'd known that in advance?". Well, you didn't, and here you are. Now it's time to start using analytics from the beginning. To test 'what-if' scenarios, model outcomes, and simulate situations. It's time to talk to people to collect the data and create your 'Management Flight Simulator'. This is the term that experts at the MIT Sloan School of Management use to describe system dynamics modeling. Remember John Sterman's book, 'Business Dynamics'? Sterman, a professor at MIT Sloan, is the greatest evangelist of using system dynamics methods for what-if scenario testing in business environments. But before we review the method, I need to explain a bit about the concept of 'cognitive maps' and the right way to 'talk to people'.

A cognitive map, or causal map, is a way to document your understanding of your situation on paper. These maps express your judgement that certain events or actions will lead to practical outcomes. If you do not have any understanding or judgment, then you head out, conduct interviews and draw the map. What is that map? It's a set of nodes linked together by relationships. At first, you need to collect the information, or conduct 'data elicitation'. A good example of data elicitation is a TV interview with a financial analyst in which he or she speaks about oil prices and speculates whether prices will go up or down. The TV host asks the analyst series of open-ended questions: 'What can cause the oil prices to change?', 'What factors control oil prices?' This unstructured data gathering – 'elicitation', or simply an interview – yields a richer understanding of a situation and important insights into existing knowledge. These probing open-ended questions can provide the TV host (or you, as the person who works on the what-if scenario testing), with a set of potential variables needed for the management flight simulator, like 'crude output rate', 'transportation cost', etc. Linkage between the map nodes can be derived from listening for words in the analyst's speech, such as 'if-then', 'because', 'so', etc. Another way to reveal relationships between the map nodes is to list all the variables and ask an expert to draw connecting links among them.

System dynamics operates using casual loop diagrams. The loops are the links between nodes that can cause the node's value to grow or to decrease. Reflecting on the oil price example, the nodes 'crude output rate' and 'transportation cost' are linked to the 'oil price' node. In general, if 'crude output rate' goes up, then the 'oil price' goes down. If an oil company manager without strategic vision wants to increase revenue during a time of decreasing prices, then he will order an increase in output in attempt to produce and sell even more oil – a decision that will cause prices to drop even lower. In system dynamics terms, this map has a reinforcing loop between the nodes. In this situation, the transportation cost can balance the oil price, since when transportation is costly then the end price is higher. The connection between these nodes on the map is called the balancing loop. Obviously, nothing can stop the TV host from asking more open-ended questions and forcing the analyst to continue speculating and adding more and more nodes and loops to the casual loop diagram. The final diagram – here, 'final' means the point when the analyst cannot add any more factors – can work as a model, or simulator, of the oil market – precisely the simulation the company managers need to test their decisions.

When programmed using specialized computer software, or even simply drawn on a whiteboard, the causal loop diagram will help you understand dynamics of your system and your business. When all the parameters are in place, you can study the stability of your decisions for vulnerability to external changes. You can identify scenarios where your business will operate in a self-sustaining mode, and ones where it will be highly unstable, when even a small breakage can cause a disaster. I'm not talking about business process modeling here – although you can surely use system dynamics for that. I'm talking about interactions between different units and even organizations inside your business.

An illustration is an Ericsson case. In the middle of the first decade of the 21st century, a lightning strike shut down a Phillips-owned semiconductor processing that was a key Ericsson supplier of mobile phone chips. Coincidently, Nokia also bought the same chips from Phillips, and the plant was the only plant Phillips had delegated for these particular semiconductor devices. In two days, news of the supply-chain problem reached Nokia's top management. Almost instantly, Nokia contacted all the relevant semiconductor device vendors to ask for help. Some agreed to adjust their processes and produce the required chips. At Ericsson, the message to the top managers traveled for three weeks from department to department, from office to office.

Finally, when the Ericsson leadership realized they had a problem, all the available manufacturers had been contracted by Nokia. Guess what? Ericsson does not produce cell phones anymore. There might be other reasons, but soon after the strike, Sony snapped up the broken Ericsson mobile division and opened the door to the mobile device market.

Managers in the Ericsson mobile division, although smart, ignored the rules of system dynamics and did not sufficiently test their business for stability. You are smarter. You know that testing 'what-if' testing scenarios is essential from the very beginning. You will not wait for the new crisis to come. You are going to build a fortress.

CHAPTER 13

DEFINITELY MAYBE

Not all data you collect after the crisis will consist of exact numbers. Not every opinion will be final. People will have doubts, you have doubts, and there will be a lot of vague talk around you. You can interview different experts and get different opinions, and even worse, similar opinions with discrepancies in details. 'Maybe yes, maybe no, maybe I don't know, plus or minus, most likely' ... you'll hear these kinds of answers all the time. As you talk to people to collect data for your new vision, you may end up lost in a mist of uncertainty. The good news is that uncertainty and probability go hand in hand. The theory of probability is a known thing you can use to blow away the smog and derive crisp answers to your questions.

Don't fear probability. It's cool. Most businesspeople are sick of hearing the word 'statistics', and tend to shrink from bell curves and strange terms like 'normal distribution' ("Why call it 'normal'?" they ask themselves). Surprisingly, the same business managers make serious faces when they hear talks about game theory and sports team management, probably because Hollywood produces movies like a 'Beautiful Mind' and 'Moneyball' to spread the word that statistics can do a lot for your business.

As before, I will not go into details, as this is not the purpose of this book. But I will give you an idea how to build cognitive maps and derive data in times of uncertainty. Causal loops in system dynamics need exact numbers, although you can build a hypothesis around the causal map structure and play what-if scenarios with it. For vague diagrams and uncertain data, you have to use Bayesian networks instead of causal loops. You may never build a Bayesian network by yourself but believe me, it's worth learning a bit about the world of Bayesian inference. After all, this algorithm describes how our brain processes information.

We are all biased towards our personal preferences.

And when we collect data, interview people, or read books, we usually have our own opinion about the situation and we change, or update that opinion as new data arrives. Amazingly, the process of updating our beliefs can be formalized using the Bayes rule and expressing it in terms of conditional probability: for any two events, A and B, $p(B|A)$ = $p(A|B) \times p(B) / p(A)$, where $p(A)$ is the probability of A, and $p(A|B)$ is the probability of A, given that B has occurred. To make it simple, the Bayes rule can be described in one sentence: by updating our initial beliefs with objective new information, we get a new and improved belief. In the charming book 'The Theory That Would Not Die', McGrayne gives plenty of examples of the Bayes rule in action, from modern spam filters to breast-cancer studies.

In Bayesian networks, fragmented knowledge from subject-matter experts is linked using Bayes rule. The Bayesian network is a map with nodes and links; formally, the network is called a 'directed acyclic graph' in which nodes represent variables, while links, or edges, represent direct causal influences among these variables. Each variable has a set of possible values called its 'state space' that consists of mutually exclusive and exhaustive values of the variable. Examples of variable states can include 'high' and 'low', 'yes' and 'no', 'good' and 'bad', etc. The beauty is that the variable value can be distributed between states. For example, if, during an interview, the oil price analyst says 'Well, if the oil prices are high, then particular customers will refuse to buy oil from this vendor' then you can link the node 'price of oil' to 'buy/not buy' node and set probability values (such as, if price is $10 per barrel, then there is a 90% chance the customers will buy the oil from this vendor). Continuing the interview, you can build and populate the Bayesian network with conditional probability values. Eventually, the network will be able to extrapolate and give you answers for questions you didn't ask the analyst or ones he didn't know the answer to. With that, you create an expert system, almost an artificial intellect that can generate answers to your questions by extrapolating the knowledge gleaned from experts and historical data. This is not science fiction. Such systems are already used to diagnose patients. Once you record the knowledge of a doctor, through a series of interviews you can input disease symptoms. The expert system will diagnose the disease and recommend a treatment. It's a helpful tool if you're in the medical business – or any other business.

With a Bayesian network, you can answer questions

that experts can't. The algorithm extrapolates between the conditional probability values and can solve a problem, even if it is new to you. When the crisis is far away and you start collecting a substantial amount of data, you can use the data to train your network, much like the black boxes in predictive analytics. Actually, the Bayesian network is a part of the predictive analytics toolbox. The difference between this and other methods such as neural networks is that we can record and input expert knowledge into it – the prior knowledge on the subject, without solid historical data. This is the power of probability theory.

During the data elicitation process (the interviews), your respondents may use different numbers to answer the same question. You can use all this information without even bothering with causal maps, diagrams, and Bayes. A method named 'Monte Carlo' is a workhorse of analysis in Excel. For example, in your crisis, a flood destroyed your business, so you decide to start an oil and gas company. Increasing oil prices convinced you that this was the right choice of business. Now you're working on a business plan, and you only have a vague idea of transportation costs. You watched a few TV shows where financial analyst mentioned different numbers for a similar environment, but you have to pick a number to place in the Excel table cell. Relax – just approximate the numbers using a distribution that fits the best, or the distribution you like the most (usually a normal distribution – the 'bell curve'.) Excel can do that. Then pick a random number out of this distribution using Excel, repeat the sampling process over and over, and your spreadsheet will be populated with outcomes covering different scenarios.

Do not afraid of vague information. Use it. There is a whole suite of analytic tools and methods ready-made for it.

CHAPTER 14

SMART SURVEYS

For your new vision, you need new data. After the crisis, you might have thought a lot and come up with a brilliant idea, but you need more data to shape it up. Talking to people and interviewing is all good and fine in the beginning. Asking open-ended questions is an exploration. The answers can surprise you, and you can learn something you might not have considered before. But what if you already know what to do? You already know your direction, you've explored a lot. Now you need detailed data you can exploit. The unstructured data from your interviews isn't enough to satisfy you. You want structured details.

Then do surveys.

In recent years, the field of business analytics for marketing has boomed and radically changed the way businesses approach their marketing investments and campaigns. Hiring managers now require employees in marketing positions to be able to speak the language of analytics and metrics, and corporate-level executives increasingly demand ROI accountability from marketing staff. However, it is not uncommon for marketers to be unfamiliar with analytics. They place themselves at a disadvantage because of their lack of knowledge. When marketers conduct surveys, usually they want to get exact numbers or exact customer preferences. Marketers are masters of business surveys. Nevertheless, for efficient surveys, you have to use analytics, and use it smartly. I personally think all surveys need to be smart.

For example, you know what business you're going to be in (since your previous idea about starting a new oil company failed). You decide to open a restaurant, or to produce new coffee machines. In any case, there are many things you'd like to know about your customers so you can match your product to their needs. I can tell you in advance that asking too many questions in one survey will not work. People will balk at answering more than 15 questions on average. Think of 15 questions as your limit. However, how can you create a survey with less than 15 questions and still collect enough data about the customer's preferences? One of the most advanced techniques for analyzing surveys is conjoint analysis, but the data collection has to thoughtful.

There are three commonly used techniques for data collection in conjoint analysis: pairwise comparison, rank ordering, and rating scale. With each of these techniques, you will have to form bundles, which represent candidate 'products' for you to test. Marketing researchers often refer to the bundles as 'cards', because research in the past used cards to represent individual bundles.

In the pairwise comparison, respondents compare two different cards with different sets of product attributes, and tell you, which attribute set they prefer. Some responders find pairwise comparison easier than rank ordering.

In rank ordering, you provide all the cards at once to the responder and ask them to rank the cards in order of preference, from their first to last choice. The advantage of rank ordering is speed, but the complexity or ordering process that the responders face is a disadvantage. Generally, responders quickly establish their most- and least-preferred choices, but find it difficult to rank the choices in the middle.

The third data collection technique is the rating scale. With this technique, you ask respondents to rate each choice on an absolute scale. The rating scale can be easier for respondents than ranking, but some of them might find it difficult to assign ratings for fine rating scales. To counter this disadvantage and to improve the consistency of results, I recommend providing guidance to respondents on how they should assign ratings to their choices, explaining in a short sentence what the particular rating means. For example, accompany a five-star rating 'outstanding' with a clarifying description like 'I will definitely buy it!'.

Conjoint analysis is a market research technique used to examine the trade-offs consumers make between product attributes. By examining the trade-offs, you can infer the value that consumers place on individual attributes. Conjoint analysis is appropriate for situations where you need to quantify customer preferences for certain attributes. The conjoint analysis process reduces preferences for certain goods and services into values, called 'part-worth', that particular attributes hold for an individual. Part-worth shows the willingness of a customer to pay for a certain attribute. Companies often use conjoint analysis in product and service development and for market segmentation. A famous example is a feature selection for a casual student bag described by Hauser, a professor at the MIT Sloan School of Management in his 'Note on Conjoint Analysis'.

A typical analysis with many attributes and many levels could result in hundreds or even thousands of combinations. To reduce the number of cards, researchers apply so-called fractional factorial techniques (for example, Taguchi orthogonal arrays). As I said before, the rule of thumb is to work with a manageable amount of cards (say, less than 15 cards).

In essence, conducting conjoint analysis has the following steps: defining the product attributes and form cards, or bundles; ask consumers to state their preferences for each bundle; code the data in a special form and conduct a regression analysis that links attributes with customer preferences; calculate the part-worths (the customer's willingness to pay for a particular attribute). The part-worths will be simply the coefficients in the regression equations, different for each respondent. However, you can combine all the regression equations into one objective function, run an optimization algorithm, and come up with an attribute set that will drive the highest revenue from the product sales.

CHAPTER 15

YOUR NICHE

Okay. You're recovering from the crisis. You talked to a number of people, thought long and hard, generated a new vision, considered what you've done wrong and what you can do better. Now it's time to find your place in the sun and lodge your business in a market niche with a good climate where your business will start to grow.

You've already conducted surveys and collected data about your customers' preferences. At first sight, the data looked scattered, and each survey response varied in some way. You faced a new challenge: to find groups of customers with similar preferences for certain product attributes, and to define your market segments.

Market segmentation is one of the tools to succeed in the market and match your competitors, who have also started to recover from the crisis. Luckily, using analytics, you can identify the groups of customers that desire your unique product or service. All markets have segments. Even commodity products, like laundry detergent, have segments: travelers prefer small packages for portability, while people with budget constraints prefer larger sizes to benefit from cheaper per-ounce prices. Identifying your market segment helps you focus your core competencies on the relevant markets and use your company resources more efficiently.

You can do market segmentation in various ways. I'll describe the most exciting method, which can help you in a way that no other method can. I'm talking about clustering. The greatest thing about clustering is that you can discover market segments without knowing anything about your market or any fine points of the business. In clustering, all you need is a database, such as survey results that someone has already collected, or even unsorted records from a supermarket cash machine. In this so-called 'post-hoc' market segmentation, you have little knowledge about the type and quantity of the segments in a particular market. The post- hoc segmentation approach determines the segments after research has been conducted and data collected. For example, a new product or service could require post-hoc segmentation techniques, because there has been no earlier consumer experience of the product.

There are two clustering methods: hierarchical and partitioning. In addition, hierarchical clustering can be agglomerative or divisive. Think of agglomerative clustering as of sticking together pieces of baker's duff. Divisive clustering is tearing the duff apart. The baker's duff itself is a metaphor for the database. Whether divisive or agglomerative, you have to decide what minimal cluster size is acceptable to you. Usually the answer comes by itself when you see the first results.

Partitioning clustering is simpler in this sense. In partitioning, you have to determine the number of clusters you want to find in the data. Much like hierarchical clustering, you can change the number of clusters as many times as you like, until the size of the cluster does not satisfy you.

There are plenty of clustering methods, and they differ in speed and accuracy. Since data volumes have grown with development of computers, new methods keep appearing on the scene. For example, a hierarchical clustering method called Ward's was known for a long time, but for basic marketing analysis IBM promoted its own hierarchical method, called TwoStep. Overall, hierarchical methods are slower than partitioning, except for IBM's TwoStep, which is implemented in IBM's SPSS software. The TwoStep clustering method can create clusters from a single data scan. Although the method has certain limitations – for example, it can be sensitive to the order of cases in the data – but it is very easy to use.

Ward's method is another popular example of agglomerative hierarchical clustering. The result of the clustering is a hierarchical structure similar to a family tree, called a dendrogram. In dendrograms, numerous tree branches merge into fewer and thicker branches until the last two merge to form a tree root. In Ward's, we start with individual elements and merge them together into clusters. During the merging process, our goal is to lose as little information as possible. For example, if we group two individuals into a cluster, the cluster will not be as precise as each individual on its own. The information lost during clustering is sometimes referred to as the merging cost. To reduce the merging cost, Ward's method minimizes the error sum of squares.

The most popular partitioning clustering method is K-means. In K-means, you simply specify K, the number of final clusters you expect, and run the algorithm. The algorithm consists of steps, which continue to iterate until a stable solution is reached. This is the moment when individual survey respondents converge into specific groups and cease to change groups. Firstly, the K-means determines so-called 'centroid coordinates' that define the center of the new segment using a weighted mean, similar to finding a center of mass in physics. The algorithm then calculates the distance of each individual object to the centroid, and forms groups based on the shortest distance. When the clusters, or market segments, form, it is up to you to accept the segmentation results or repeat the analysis using other parameters. There's no silver bullet here.

Imagine you decided to be in the coffee-machine business. You conducted a market survey and did some conjoint analysis. You ended up with a database full of part-worths from individual survey respondents. Now is the time to apply clustering and to find your market segments. You designed the survey to reveal preferences for females and males who work at home or in an office, weighted against the price, speed, and size of the coffee machine. The clustering algorithm, applied to part-worths (or willingness to pay), found two distinct sets of respondents: females working in an office with a high willingness to pay for the speed of the coffee machine and low part-worths for the price itself; and male working from home with high part-worths for the machine volume and a low willingness to pay for an expensive product. Using this knowledge, you can identify your market segments: fast and premium coffee machines for women at work, and high-capacity, budget machines for men working at home.

Always collect data as much as possible. Collect, record, store and analyze. Your efforts will pay off.

CHAPTER 16

THE SIMS

This method is the cherry on top – the most advanced. Actually, it's so advanced that there is still no theory around it, although it is used effectively in practice. The method is agent-based modeling.

We talked about simulating business processes on a computer using all the process details, product line parts, elevators, forklift trucks, etc. So why not extend the idea of simulation to people – your customers, your vendors, your truck drivers, your corporate personnel? The major difference between simulating the forklift truck in your warehouse using discrete event modeling versus agent-based modeling is that the latter method includes the truck driver – an autonomous decision entity, an agent, a human being, who needs a lunch break, who works in shifts, who is exposed to other human factors, who has friends. You may not bother about the forklift truck driver's friends, but you should consider social networks if you're interested in marketing companies, the market adoption of new products, or the diffusion of innovation. Before talking about social networks, I will illustrate the method through a simple problem that you'd have trouble solving through means other than agent-based modeling.

The example involves road traffic. If you're the city's mayor, you want to get rid of traffic jams. You can direct your city transportation department to test various road systems and stoplight timing in a virtual world, in your Sim-City build with agent-based technology, where all drivers make independent decisions about their speed and route. This is not an exotic example – this is real-world stuff. Agent-based modeling is used for traffic-pattern testing in complex environments like airports. Frankfurt airport, one of Europe's busiest airports, runs a decision support system based on agent-based modeling. How about that?

Here's an example from advertising. You run an agency that manages billboards in Piccadilly Circus, a place full of people and cars in the heart of London. How do you set the rental prices for various boards? By their size? What is your reasoning? The billboard's rental price has to be linked to the number of people who see it, just as search engines charge according to the number of the ad impressions. How else can you get these numbers other than by creating a 'Sim City' with Piccadilly Circus and 'asking' your virtual inhabitants, pedestrians and drivers how frequently they see a particular banner? That is doable. As source data, you can use street cams and plans of the actual square and adjacent roads.

Yes, I know. This book is about anti-crisis analytics, the business analytics that help before, during, and after a crisis. This part of the book is about methods that can help your business recover after the crisis. The major attribute of an economy after a crisis is an absence of historical data. You have to know how the market will react to your product, what market share you can count on, and what the best design for a marketing campaign might be, but all your experience is often irrelevant because the world is new. The world is new, but the rules of life are the same. People sleep, eat, go to work, marry, divorce, read and watch the news using various technologies. Their basic needs are still there.

You can simulate your business environment, you customer behavior, your market, by creating an agent-based world. There are consulting companies, books, conferences, and whole suites of computer software for that. Eric Bonabeau, with his book 'Swarm Intelligence: From Natural to Artificial Systems', is one of the pioneers who commercialized agent-based modeling.

I said there is no theory around agent-based modeling. Why? The method itself is clear and straightforward to implement, but there is a hidden power that scientists cannot yet understand. At some point, the agent-based model will generate answers that are robust and trustworthy, but counterintuitive. This effect is called the emergent phenomenon – the situation when a system consisting of simple elements demonstrates a complex behavior that none of its agents have on their own. The shoal of fish can fool a predator, or a flock of birds can find food for everyone, although in both cases the individual participants just watch their nearest neighbors and move in the same direction. The Boston Museum of Science has a great exhibit on swarm intelligence that uses gaming computers where you can change the behavior of individual agents and watch how the whole system grows or falls apart.

If you're not in the fishing business, you may not care about shoals at all. But how about marketing strategies for a new, unique, and innovative product that you invented after the crisis? How about agent-based modeling of the diffusion of innovation? This is the term marketers use to describe market adoption of a new product. It captures complex system phenomena related to social-network topology, in contrast to traditional approaches such as Fisher-Pry or Bass models. These effects can be crucial for accurate prediction of market adoption rates in markets where the influence of word-of-mouth is strong.

The consumer decision-making process for new product adoption involves a complex interaction of various external and internal factors including mass media, advertising, word-of-mouth, personal preferences and experience. Interpersonal communications, without a doubt, constitute an important communication media, especially for social groups that are hard to reach through mass-media advertising. A friend's opinion or advice often could be a decisive argument for a purchase. If you want to provide accurate and reliable estimations of diffusion of innovation rates, you shouldn't neglect the existence and structure of the social network of your potential customers (your product adopters).

When the individual behavior patterns of the product adopters are similar, you can describe their social neighborhood topology as a random network where each person has an equal number of peers or friends. For example, you can use random networks in behavior studies of large societies, like a state or country, where the personal characteristics of each particular individual make no difference.

You can use other types of social networks, a scale-free, highly non-homogenous network, where certain persons, called hubs, have the ability to reach a large number of people while others have only few connections. Sales professionals and hiring agents are examples of such social hubs. Real-world social networks can be a mixture of these two extreme cases and can depend on the type of product.

For your market simulation, you can take several typical customer profiles to create agents, and then clone them using slight random variations in parameters like age and income until you reach the size of the city. A million agents? No problem. Using modern software, you can simulate the behavior of a market consisting of millions of virtual customers on your laptop!

One of the counterintuitive effects found during diffusion-of-innovation studies is that in random networks the diffusion of innovation accelerates significantly when the population is split into clusters. For example, if you want to sell your product in two neighboring cities, then start selling it in one of the cities, not in both. The resulting adoption rate will be almost twice as high. The finding here is that people look at their friends to check whether they have the product or not. Friends who bought the product and live in the same city as you are closer to you socially, and will be convinced faster. The second city will adopt your product almost instantly when the citizens see that everyone in their neighboring city already has your product.

But enough of stories! It's time for action. It is time to set up your business analytics.

One More Thing:

Your Business Analytics

CHAPTER 17

YOUR DATA

The worst thing you can do is to store your data in Excel spreadsheets. It's okay to store some data there, but don't routinely store all your sales, process, and other kinds of data in tables that are scattered across drives, with misprints of variable names and no tracking tags. There are fairly large barriers to installing a data collection system, so business owners often hesitate to do it. As a result, they increase the costs of run installing a business analytics system in the future. This situation is analogous to the installation of enterprise resource planning (ERP) systems like SAP in 1990s. Everyone understood that their business needed IT to manage their processes, and the tree of competition forced them to do it (remember 'Introduction' section?). The SAP installations were extremely expensive. For a mid-sized plant, the transfer of documents to an electronic format could cost several million dollars and last from one to two years. This was not because SAP was expensive – it was because the documentation flow and interactions between the departments was a mess. Cleaning it up and bringing the process up to standard was the most time- and money-consuming part.

Sooner or later, the law of competitive evolution will force you to store and analyze your data to stay in the game – just as SAP and similar systems did in the last decade of the twentieth century. When this day comes, your pain will be so strong that even millions of dollars will not help. If you weren't already collecting data in the proper way, then you will be at the end of the line by definition. Your competitors, who were accurately recording and properly storing their process data, will be far ahead of you in their predictive capabilities.

If you are still using Excel spreadsheets, then at least follow these three rules:

Rule 1:

Always store separate variables in separate columns. Always!

Rule 2:

Each row is a record. Your table must be nice and clean.

Rule 3:

You first variable is date. Your second variable is the origin of the data. Then comes the rest.

Start with these three rules. Talk to your team, and introduce a culture of data storage. Force them to participate. They will be reluctant, but they'll get used to it – and it will save you a lot of money in the future.

This is just the start. You cannot continue using Excel for much longer and here's a simple example to illustrate why. Say your sales representative records his sales according to the three rules, and one variable is the customer's name. If you want to learn more about that customer, then you have to look up a card with his profile, presumably in a separate table stored somewhere. These two tables are related – but there is no good way to create relational tables in Excel. If you have thousands of customers, you simply must use relational databases. The upshot is that you will inevitably use databases, and you will have to train your personnel about the concept of relational databases beforehand. They should not afraid of databases, and they should understand the meaning of the word 'database'. I have seen a number of cases where people have called Excel tabs a 'database'. In the modern world, those who are afraid of databases and don't know how to deal with them look like people who afraid of printers in early '80s and used typewriters.

Databases accept data through forms. There are several ways to submit data to a database, but you can think of the database interface as a web form. By the way, all websites use databases to store data. Play with Microsoft Access to get an idea of what databases look like. You don't have to become an Access expert – but at least launch it!

When you accept the fact that you cannot avoid using databases in your business, read the 'Database Normalization' article on Wikipedia. You'll learn about database structure, reference keys, and SQL abbreviation. SQL stands for Structured Query Language. You don't have to know it, but you have to know it exists. SQL is the primary language for dealing with databases and storing and retrieving data. All this is common knowledge you need in the new digital era. You may drive your car without knowing much about its parts, but at least you have an idea of what the transmission does. At a minimum, you know that it's a part of your car. The same goes for SQL and databases – you have to know about SQL's existence, and you have to have the technology in your business. There are different types of database designs and vendors, and SQL is not the only technology – but leave that stuff to the technical experts.

CHAPTER 18

YOUR SOFTWARE

Be serious about your software from the beginning. I am making comparisons with cars all the time, so, think of your software like your car. Each time you take your place in front of the steering wheel, you entrust your life to the machine. To a great extent, you entrust the existence of your business to software. There are myriads of software companies, start-ups, university spin-offs, and open-source codes that provide the functionality needed for business analytics. Ignore it. Work only with the giants. Some open-source software might be perfect, most start-up software will be cheaper, some will provide you with dedicated support. None of this matters. The essential thing here is the company's reliability. Do you want your business to last for 20 years? Then chose a vendor that already proved to be on the market for 20 years. When you will filter the list, only three companies will remain: IBM, Microsoft, and SAS.

At this point, you're ready to be introduced to the terms 'structured' and 'unstructured' data. Simply put, tables contain structured data. If you have only tables, and images of similar format (such as photos of your customers, pictures of your products, or scans of related documents) then use SQL-type databases. Microsoft is good for these. On the other hand, if you have a disk drive full of miscellaneous files, then your data is unstructured. The Internet is an enormous reservoir of unstructured data. Your 'My Documents' folder stores unstructured data. There are few operations you can do with unstructured data. Basically, you can only search it. If your volumes are huge, and you are going to search for texts and images, then use Hadoop- type storage. Formally, Hadoop is not a database, but a file system that works well – and quickly – on large data volumes. Have you heard the term 'Big Data'? This term mostly describes unstructured data like audio, video, images, and unsorted texts. IBM is good for sorting through that. There are SQL solutions for unstructured data by Teradata, so contact them if you operate with both structured and unstructured data. (Do you?)

Most of the time, your business will work with an SQL database. In that case, I recommend that you use Microsoft to build your predictive analytics system. They offer everything. Microsoft SQL Server can store and retrieve data, analyze it, and generate reports. The Analytics Services of MS SQL Server is so powerful that it even has neural networks and Bayesian networks under the Microsoft brand. You can plug this data server into Microsoft's native reporting system, SharePoint, which is document management software, but also an excellent and powerful reporting tool with a web interface. (Microsoft uses the word 'power' everywhere, as in PowerView, PowerPivot, and PowerQuery, for example.)

IBM has all of the tools. Actually, even more tools than Microsoft, since they have IBM SPSS, a world-standard tool for business statistics. SPSS is one of the few commercial multi-purpose packages with a dedicated function for conjoint analysis, although it is not well documented. A big plus is that IBM's tools have graphical interfaces. If in Microsoft SQL Server you have to write a program to set up your predictive analytics, in IBM you can do it through a graphical user interface (but, of course, you can also program it). For example, IBM SPSS Modeler is a user-friendly tool that's as good for express analysis as it is for a production system. However, once you create a production system, you won't care how was it created (i.e., through programing or via mouse manipulations).

Speaking of statistics, I cannot ignore SAS. SAS started with statistics and gained credibility with its flagship product, 'SAS' (the same as the company name). The pharmaceutical industry often uses SAS to process data from clinical trials. Lately, the company decided to expand into the broader field of business analytics, which requires interfaces with data storage and reporting capabilities. To me, the only reason to use SAS is legacy data and compatibility. If you already have something written in SAS, then you can consider this option. If not, then check out their 'JMP' software. This is one of the best applications for regression analysis, basic data mining, and data visualization. And it's cheap.

There are number of other software packages for predictive analytics. If you want to save money use Rapid Miner (it looks like IBM's SPSS Modeler) or use 'R' software, or any free SQL database with reasonable documentation. For example, MySQL's database is a reasonably safe place to land. It is originally from Sweden, now owned by Oracle, and free.

For the other business analytics methods I mentioned in this book, there is no gold standard. For all kinds of business process modeling, try AnyLogic, which is modern and well-supported software. AnyLogic is flexible and includes both system dynamics and agent-based modeling. However, for system dynamics alone you will be fine with VenSim, an application developed at MIT. It is very handy. For agent-based modeling, you will probably need an expert. You can play with NetLogo, and read about Repast, but if you are open-minded and decide to use agents – find an expert. Most likely, you will need to write a new system from scratch.

For the rest, you will find everything you need in IBM, Microsoft, and SAS software suites.

CHAPTER 19

YOUR PEOPLE

Last but not the least, are your people. You heard it right – your people come last in this sequence, right after data collection and software. However, at the head of them all is you, the visionary, the person who oversees the whole business and understands the roles of your various personnel. Understanding roles is an important. As you learned in this book, business analytics is not just about business processes, or sales forecasting, or data management and reporting. Business analytics is just the umbrella concept. This is the new age of competition. To me, job postings that say 'We need a business analyst' make no sense. People often confuse business analytics with business process analysis. To them, a business analyst is just another name for a business process analyst. They also think that 'business analysts' are system integrators, database administrators, project managers, financial analysts, marketing analysis, sales analysts, and other specialized experts in different fields.

If you're looking for a new hire to help you with business analytics, don't use 'business analyst' in the job title. You need an expert in your particular field who possesses business analytics skills. If you're in the banking industry, you need a financial analyst with business analytics skills. If you're in consumer goods, you may need a marketer with business analytics skills. If you want to improve your business process, you need a process engineer with business analytics skills or an expert in business process optimization. 'Business analytics skills' implies knowledge of system dynamics, databases and data mining. If you appeal for help to a company that provides business analytics services, you have to delegate an expert within your business domain to work together with the company's people.

Epilogue

There is a classic recipe for surviving a crisis. You have to accumulate cash while you can – the cash that will nourish you through your financial hunger. You have to invest into R&D and routinely improve your processes – Japanese call this *kaizen* – to change for the better. You have to keep your savings, investments, and debts in healthy balance. You need to know your escape route in advance, the 'rings of defense' you will deploy when the crisis hits. You have to have a portfolio of businesses in independent industries, and you need to learn how to prioritize your projects and get rid of toxic assets. This is a huge burden to carry as an executive. You understand that you must rely on data while making decisions, because, as we all know 'words are cheap'. These days, ignoring data is not an option, because your rivals are always exploring new ways to compete.

The history of competition, which I depict as a tree, teaches us that the way companies differentiate themselves changes over time. Ancient artisans appealed to beauty and quality, conveyers and production lines dramatically reduced costs, management science increased efficiency, information technology accelerated processes, and business analytics made competitive foresight a commodity.

Sun Tzu, the author of 'The Art of War', wrote that "the battle is won before it's ever fought." This wisdom can now serve as a guideline for every modern company. As before, most decisions are based on forecasts, except today's forecasts are based on data and generated by computers. Incorporating business analytics into your business will strengthen you before a crisis, help you to survive during the crisis, and jump-start your operations after the crisis has passed.

Before a crisis, try to forecast as much as possible. Use predictive analytics wherever you have data. None of your data storage should operate without a black box that searches for correlations and predicts the next value. And none of your business units should operate without digital records and databases for data storage. Predictive analytics will reveal patterns in your business, detect deviations long before a human eye can do it, and spot stagnations that should send warning signals about upcoming disruptive change – i.e., a crisis.

During the crisis, improve and optimize. Streamline your business processes, remove bottlenecks, minimize non-value-added steps, work hard to deliver quick turnaround and zero delays. Make the process robust and stable in order to maintain supply, with zero variability and optimal product quality. This is tough, but you have to do it. Business process modeling is the key to performance excellence. When you are short on budget, people, materials, machines – you should optimize, explore and exploit, and find the best combination of these elements with the help of algorithms.

After a crisis, the world is never the same, and most experience is irrelevant. Talk to people, conduct interviews and surveys, build cognitive maps and causal loops, use system dynamics and simulations, and run what-if scenarios. Collect every piece of information, don't be afraid of vague data, cluster and structure your findings using analytics, find your market niche and your ideal set of product attributes – and start growing from there.

Be serious about data collection and analytics

software from the start. Educate your employees about the culture of data storage, and teach them how to use databases (or at least explain the basics). Avoid open-source code, free software, start-ups and fresh university spin-offs. Choose vendors you can rely on – i.e., those with at least a proven, 20-year record of market success. Use 'all-in-one' software suites that include data storage, data analysis, and reporting. Your business analytics system should be rock-solid, not something built from fragments and pieces.

Don't mess with the terms. Don't call everything 'Big Data'. You have to clearly understand the new professions and job descriptions. Marketing analyst, sales analyst, financial analyst, system analyst, business process analyst – these are all different experts. Business analytics is a set of skills and technologies, not a profession by itself. You have to remember this fact when you will start implementing business analytics in your company.

Thank you for reading this book. I hope I have planted a seed and that we all experience fewer crises in the future. I deeply acknowledge my editor Alec Ross for polishing the text and all my friends and co-workers for sharing their thoughts – and for challenging mine.

Lev Kuandykov, March 2015